JANE HARRIS

PAINTINGS AND DRAWINGS

with essays by Martin Hentschel and Godfrey Worsdale

23:39 Pencil on Fabriano paper 2000 57x76cm

Drawings?
Godfrey Worsdale

When considering the central tenets of draughtsmanship, first amongst them is the notion of conception. Drawing, beyond the basic physical act of pulling a line out of matter, has always been recognised as a means of conceiving and visualising an idea. Indeed, during the Italian Renaissance the term *disegno* had, as its two most fundamental definitions, drawing and design. By tradition artists, along with inventors, engineers, designers and architects, begin their creative operations at the drawing board. It is often at this moment that many of the most significant images in visual culture are manufactured. It is also the point at which the artist's ideas are most unfettered by conscious process and issues of reception; a degree of freedom is sustained that facilitates the generation of a pure visualised thought. The act of manufacture thereafter can be pursued in any number of ways but all of them must be consequent to and reliant on, the first draught.

Jane Harris has, of late, begun to produce drawings that make a departure from this traditional understanding. The series of works illustrated here, though made with the most basic materials, represent a nonconformist approach to the production of drawings. In physical essence the works are created by applying pencil onto paper but beyond that, they very persuasively resist the experimental, investigative and curious position that is introduced above. Harris' drawings are calculated in the extreme. The only irresolute element in the process is the way in which these creations might be intelligible to the viewer, ie, how they might function as the visual communication of information or ideas. These drawings are predetermined to such an extent that their realisation almost feigns an absence of artistic intervention, that they came about by some other means. There is a strong sense in these works that they are not intended to disclose their means of production readily. This is not to imply some kind of deception in their production and presentation, rather to generate an understanding of these drawings as phenomenological entities. As such, this work is as capable of surprising the viewer, as it is able to reassure through its resolve. In an analysis of this work it is within such oppositional qualities that the drawings inevitably function and find their momentum.

In real terms, these drawings present themselves as a series of creative artistic statements, albeit somewhat closed and composed. At the same moment however, this interpretation is directly contrasted by the mechanical and quasi-mathematical detachment that seems to account for the works realisation. Similarly, whilst at one moment the forms that exist within these images are clearly contrivances of conscious invention they also make a forceful claim to

---

Zeichnungen?
Godfrey Worsdale

Wenn wir nach den Grundelementen der Zeichenkunst fragen, ist an erster Stelle der Begriff der Vorstellung zu nennen. Abgesehen vom zu Grunde liegenden physischen Akt des Ziehens einer Linie aus Materie ist das Zeichnen seit jeher als ein Mittel zur Konzeption und Visualisierung einer Idee angesehen worden. In der italienischen Renaissance hatte der Begriff "disegno" tatsächlich zweierlei Grundbedeutungen, nämlich "Zeichnung" und "Entwurf". Traditionell begann der bildende Künstler ebenso wie der Erfinder, der Ingenieur, der Designer oder der Architekt seine schöpferische Arbeit am Zeichenbrett. Dies ist der Moment, in dem vielfach die bedeutendsten Hervorbringungen der Bildkultur geboren werden. Zugleich ist dies der Punkt, an dem die Ideen des Künstlers am wenigsten getrübt sind durch bewusste Vorgänge und Fragen der Rezeption: Es besteht ein Maß an Freiheit, das die Hervorbringung eines reinen visualisierten Gedankens erleichtert. Der Akt der Herstellung kann daraufhin auf jede nur denkbare Art und Weise erfolgen, nur dass sie sich aus dem ersten Entwurf ergeben und auf diesen stützen muss.

Jane Harris hat in jüngster Zeit angefangen, Zeichnungen zu machen, die von diesem herkömmlichen Verständnis abrücken. Der hier abgebildete Zyklus von Arbeiten stellt, obwohl unter Verwendung der elementarsten Materialien gefertigt, eine nonkonformistische Herangehensweise an die Schaffung von Zeichnungen dar. Von ihrer materiellen Grundlage her entstehen die Arbeiten zwar durch das Aufsetzen eines Bleistifts auf Papier, darüber hinaus jedoch widersetzen sie sich sehr überzeugend dem oben angerissenen experimentellen, forschenden Prinzip. Die Zeichnungen von Jane Harris sind extrem kalkuliert. Das einzige unentschiedene Element ist dabei, wie diese Schöpfungen für den Betrachter verständlich sein könnten, das heißt wie sie im Sinne der visuellen Kommunikation von Information oder Ideen funktionieren könnten. Die Zeichnungen sind in einem Maße prädeterminiert, dass ihre Ausführung nachgerade ein Nichtvorhandensein künstlerischer Intervention vorspiegelt, als seien sie auf irgendeine andere Art und Weise zu Stande gekommen. Die Arbeiten vermitteln den starken Eindruck, als seien sie nicht dazu gedacht, ihre Entstehungsweise ohne weiteres preiszugeben. Damit soll nicht suggeriert werden, bei ihrer Entstehung und Präsentation sei irgendeine Art der Täuschung im Spiel, sondern vielmehr ein Verständnis für die Zeichnungen als phänomenologische Entitäten geweckt werden. Als solche vermögen die Arbeiten den Betrachter ebenso sehr zu überraschen, wie sie ihn durch ihre Vorsätzlichkeit zu beruhigen vermögen. In einer Analyse dieses Schaffens sind es unweigerlich Polaritäten dieser Art, im Rahmen derer die Zeichnungen funktionieren und ihre volle Wirkung entfalten.

some sense of natural evolution. This paradoxical interpretation is extended further within the relationship between the visual and physical nature of the work. Whist, as will be argued further, the work maintains a strong illusory quality, it is also brought about by a powerfully sculpted process which scrutinises the physicality of both paper and pencil. To an extent, the very texture and imperial sized proportions of the Fabriano paper that is used exclusively in the production of these works, makes them in part, ready made. The movement of the pencil thereafter, navigates the characteristic inconsistencies of the surface with a definite purpose, both exploiting and enhancing these qualities whilst ultimately rendering them inconsequential in the eventual achievement of a true description of form. As a corollary to this, an illusion of tension is established between the medium and its support. The pencil graphite, which is so laboriously forced into contact with the surface of the sheet, then seems to exist both as some kind of shallow atmosphere above the whiteness of the paper and as deep space behind it. The visual sense that one makes of these works, therefore, can be either a physical one or an illusory one but the discordance of the two positions is perhaps the central charge to a unified visual engagement with these objects.

Above and beyond a physical analysis of these objects, for they are as much physical as they are pictorial, the central visual concern is surely a formal one, and this consideration is dominated in each and every case by the duality of the compositions. As a result of the issues reflected upon above, there is a question about the relationship between the two forms and their ability to function as a plausible singular and unified composition. This is heightened by the potential for each form to operate in its own right, isolated in a separate part of the sheet. Whilst one could determine the works as being the presentation of two related but independent forms, it is also reasonable to be occupied by the implications that one form has for the other. As a classic modernist device the notion of contrapuntal forms is by no means a new one. Nor, however, is it a concern unknown to physicists who are occupied by the forces that simultaneously attract and repel pairs of bodies, from the molecular to the stellar. By the intensity of her use of materials, Harris is able to create a delusion of mass, which effectively harnesses our understanding of these forces. The forms are juxtaposed to the same extent that they are counterposed and with this, the dynamic is established.

Visually, the coupling of these forms provides a balance that accentuates the sense of resolve discussed but there are also implications for the way in which one sees the individual elements. Neither part can exist in isolation but at the same time, nor can their clear isolation on the surface of the sheet be disregarded. Optically the implications of this are twofold. Initially one's attention is pulled from side to side, establishing the symmetry or asymmetry that may

Konkret gesagt, stellen die Zeichnungen sich dar als eine Reihe künstlerisch-schöpferischer Statements, wenn auch ein wenig gerichtet und gezügelt. Gleichzeitig jedoch wird diese Einschätzung unmittelbar konterkariert durch die mechanische, scheinbar mathematische Leidenschaftslosigkeit der Ausführung, die für die Arbeiten kennzeichnend zu sein scheint. In gleicher Weise nehmen die Form- oder Bildelemente in den Zeichnungen, während sie einerseits offensichtlich das Produkt bewusster Erfindung sind, andererseits nachdrücklich eine Art von natürlicher Evolution für sich in Anspruch. Diese Paradoxie setzt sich fort innerhalb der Beziehung zwischen dem visuellen und dem materiellen Charakter der Arbeiten. Während die Arbeiten, wie noch darzulegen sein wird, einen betont illusorischen Charakter wahren, kommen sie gleichzeitig zu Stande durch einen ausgesprochen bildhauerischen Vorgang, der die Materialität von Papier wie Bleistift auslotet. In gewisser Weise machen schon die Beschaffenheit des Papiers der Marke Fabriano, das für sämtliche dieser Arbeiten Verwendung findet, und die britischen Maße der Blätter sie zu Teil-Ready-mades. Der Weg, den sich daraufhin der Bleistift bahnt, führt ganz gezielt entlang den typischen Unregelmäßigkeiten der Oberfläche, die gleichzeitig ausgenützt und betont werden, während ihnen schließlich im Zuge der letztendlichen Realisierung einer in sich stimmigen Formbeschreibung jede Bedeutung wieder genommen wird. Infolgedessen ergibt sich eine Illusion der Spannung zwischen Zeichenmittel und Bildträger. Der Graphit des Bleistifts, der mit so viel Mühe der Oberfläche des Blattes aufgedrückt wird, scheint dann gleichzeitig in einer Art untiefer Atmosphäre über der Weiße des Papiers zu existieren und wie tiefer Raum dahinter. Das Bild, das man sich von diesen Arbeiten macht, kann folglich entweder ein materielles sein oder ein illusorisches, es ist jedoch die Divergenz dieser beiden Positionen, die den vielleicht wichtigsten Anstoß zu einer übergreifenden Seherfahrung der Objekte abgibt.

Über eine rein materielle Analyse dieser Objekte hinaus, denn sie sind ja tatsächlich ebenso materiell wie bildnerisch, ist das zentrale visuelle Moment sicherlich ein formales, wobei in jedem einzelnen Fall die Dualität der Komposition bestimmend ist. Infolge der oben erörterten Sachverhalte stellt sich die Frage nach der Beziehung zwischen den beiden Formen und nach deren Glaubwürdigkeit als in sich zusammenhängender Komposition. Dies wird noch verstärkt durch die Tatsache, dass jede Form, jeweils für sich in einem eigenen Teil des Blattes angeordnet, tatsächlich für sich selbst zu bestehen vermag. Während man einerseits zu dem Schluss kommen könnte, dass es bei den Arbeiten um die Präsentation zweier miteinander in Zusammenhang stehender, jedoch unabhängiger Formen gehe, ist es andererseits ebenso angemessen, sich mit der Frage zu befassen, welche Implikationen die eine Form für die andere hat. Als ein klassisches Bildmittel der Moderne ist das Prinzip kontrapunktischer Formen keineswegs neu. Ebensowenig ist es Physikern fremd, die sich mit den Kräften der Anziehung und Abstoßung zwischen zwei

exist between the pair of forms. This is arrested with the second visual consequence that is derived from the distinguishing details with which each of the basically ovoid forms is characterised. Though the manipulations of the forms are usually balanced on either side, they inevitably snag the eye as one seeks to contemplate the whole.

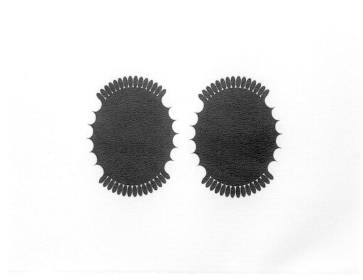

6:15 Pencil on Fabriano paper 2000 57x76cm (Private collection)

When seen as a body of works these manipulations can run together to animate the same basic foundation. In this sense, this work recreates the model by which we already visually understand and rationalise the world. As trees in a forest for instance, are each accepted as being the same, we can be sure that they will all be uniquely distinct natural occurrences, so too are these works endorsed by their individual manipulations. This leads one to consider Harris' work in the currently topical contexts of cloning and genetic modification. As one moves from work to work they pursue one particular formal direction for a number of images before following another tangent. The ovoid form might swell to almost circular proportions before being stretched into a slender torpedo shape. A fringe of small round protrusions may develop into a line for thrusting blade-like fingers or alternatively they may become the very negative of their own form, defining the spaces previously between. As a consequence, the viewer is always left with a sense of curiosity as to the direction of the

Körpern, von molekularen bis hin zu stellaren, beschäftigen. Kraft der Intensität, mit der sie ihr Material einsetzt, schafft es Harris, eine Illusion der Masse zu erzeugen, die tatsächlich unser Verständnis dieser Kräfte prägt. Die Formen sind in gleichem Maße einander an die Seite wie einander gegenübergestellt, und eben daraus ergibt sich die Dynamik.

Optisch gesehen sorgt die Paarung dieser Formen für ein Gleichgewicht, das den erwähnten Eindruck der Vorsätzlichkeit unterstreicht. Zugleich jedoch hat dies Folgen für die Art und Weise, wie wir die einzelnen Elemente sehen. Keines der beiden Teile kann für sich alleine existieren, es sei denn zu gleicher Zeit. Ebenso unmöglich aber ist es, ihre offensichtliche Isolierung auf der Oberfläche des Blattes zu ignorieren. Für das Auge ergibt sich daraus zweierlei: Zunächst wird der Blick von einer Seite zur anderen gezogen, wodurch sich die etwaige Symmetrie oder Asymmetrie zwischen dem Formenpaar ergibt. Die zweite Folge aber ist die, dass der Blick angehalten wird durch die unterschiedlichen Detailmerkmale, die die beiden im Wesentlichen ovoiden Formen kennzeichnen. Obwohl sich die gestalterischen Eingriffe in die Grundform auf beiden Seiten in der Regel die Waage halten, ziehen sie unweigerlich den Blick auf sich, wenn man versucht, das Ganze in Augenschein zu nehmen. Im Zusammenhang der Werkgruppe betrachtet, können diese gestalterischen Eingriffe im Zusammenspiel zur Belebung ein und desselben zu Grunde liegenden Elementes führen. In diesem Sinn reproduzieren die Arbeiten das Modell, nach dem wir die Welt ohnehin optisch erfassen und rationalisieren. So wie der einzelne Baum im Wald den übrigen Bäumen gleichgesetzt wird, obwohl gleichzeitig kein Zweifel daran bestehen kann, dass jeder Baum eine einzigartige Hervorbringung der Natur ist, so beziehen diese Arbeiten ihre Identität aus ihren jeweiligen gestalterischen Eingriffen. Dies legt es nahe, Harris' Werk vor dem Hintergrund der heute aktuellen Diskussion über das Klonen und genetische Manipulation zu betrachten. In den Arbeiten wird über eine Folge von Blättern hinweg eine bestimmte formale Richtung verfolgt, bist ein anderer Seitenweg weiterverfolgt wird. Die Eiform kann zu nahezu kreisförmigen Abmessungen anschwellen, um anschließend zu einer schmalen Torpedoform gestreckt zu werden. Ein Rand aus kleinen runden Ausbuchtungen kann sich zu einer Linie entwickeln, die ausgestreckte klingenartige Finger beschreibt, oder statt der Ausbuchtungen können auch die Zwischenräume zwischen ihnen umrissen werden, so dass sich ein genaues Negativbild ergibt. Infolgedessen bewahrt der Betrachter immer eine Neugier darauf, in welche Richtung die Arbeit gehen wird. Die Möglichkeiten sind von der Anlage her unbegrenzt, und dennoch ist das Endspiel bei diesen Arbeiten zumindest etwas, das fesselt. Der Künstlerin gelingt es, die Arbeiten freizuhalten von jeglichem linearen Begriff des Fortschritts: Sie stellen vielmehr eine Reihe von Manövern innerhalb eines bestimmten Feldes dar. Ungeachtet dessen sind es gerade die Möglichkeiten, die sich für die Weiterentwicklung oder den Abschluss

work. The options are potentially endless and yet the end game for this work is at the very least, a source of intrigue. The artist is able to conceive of these works as being without a linear sense of progression, rather that they represent a series of manoeuvres within a given field. Despite this the very potential for the eventual evolution or cessation of this body of work is in itself engaging. The drawings manifest themselves as the antidote to their own anxieties. The limitless potential for new variants is held in check by the meticulousness of the resolve of each individual production. Each new form thrives on its uniquely defining features and yet is repeated, or mirrored, on the same sheet of paper. Paradoxically, none of these forms is perfect and yet each of them is faultless. The materials are deployed in a way devised, in part, to overcome their own reality, enabling the artist to manufacture something that alludes to be much more than a combination of its component elements.

These works, which enjoy an engaging relationship to Harris' paintings, to some degree represent the full extent of her position. Her work has always reflected on ideas of control and sensation, facility and aesthetics, and in this recent body of works on paper these issues have been considered with great elegance and an almost diagrammatic rigour.

dieser Werkgruppe bieten, die faszinieren. Die Zeichnungen offenbaren sich als das Gegenmittel zu ihren eigenen Ängsten. Das unbegrenzte Potential für neue Varianten wird eingedämmt durch die Akribie der Vorsätzlichkeit jeder einzelnen Hervorbringung. Jede neue Form lebt von der Einzigartigkeit ihrer besonderen Merkmale, und dennoch wird sie auf dem gleichen Blatt Papier wiederholt oder auch gespiegelt. Paradoxerweise ist keine dieser Formen vollkommen, und doch ist jede einzelne fehlerlos. Die Materialien werden eingesetzt in einer Art und Weise, die nicht zuletzt dazu dient, ebenderen Realität zu überwinden: Dies erlaubt es der Künstlerin, etwas herzustellen, das suggeriert, viel mehr zu sein als eine Summe seiner Teile.

In diesen Arbeiten, die in einer interessanten Zusammenhang zu ihren Gemälden stehen, kristallisiert sich bis zu einem gewissen Grad die künstlerische Position von Jane Harris. Ihre Arbeit kreist seit jeher um Fragen der Kontrolle und des Gefühls, der Leichtigkeit und der Ästhetik, und in diesem jüngsten Zyklus von Arbeiten auf Papier sind diese Themen mit besonderer Eleganz und einer beinahe diagrammatischen Stringenz behandelt worden.

Translation: Bram Opstelten

23:38 Pencil on Fabriano paper 2000 57x76cm

22:31 2000 Pencil on Fabriano paper 57x76cm (Private collection)

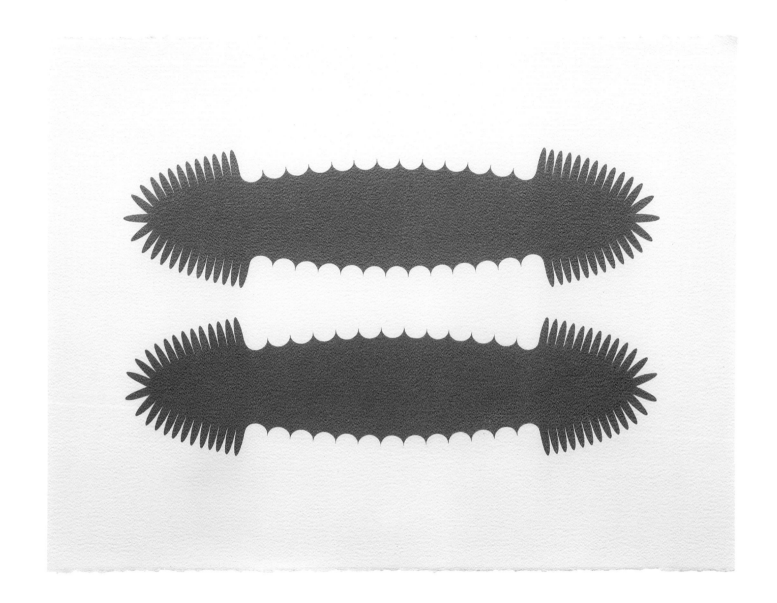

13:26 2000 Pencil on Fabriano paper 57x76cm

12:24 2000 Pencil on Fabriano paper 57x76cm

3:21 2000 Pencil on Fabriano paper 57x76cm

Bloody Mary 2000 Oil on canvas 158x153cm

Transforming Geometry and Ornament - On the Paintings of Jane Harris
Martin Hentschel

I think that above everything else a painting should be an ornament - Maurice Denis 1893[1]

I The Discomfiture of Ornament

The beginnings of abstract art, as Ernst Gombrich has demonstrated, are indebted to a sustained debate on ornament and decoration, but once enthroned, it speedily disavowed these roots. The reason lay in the traditional view of ornament as appended form. No matter how multiform and daring its vocabulary, it was always beholden to an order with its own defining criteria. Ornament covering an architectonic structure would conceal or accentuate it, but it always retained its nature as an embellishing detail or secondary feature. With regard to the organisation of traditional painting, the applicative function was obvious. Ornament was free to unfold even in a frame, but the frame was not necessarily linked to one and the same picture. It could be exchanged from owner to owner.

Philip Otto Runge may well have been the first modern artist to revaluate the subordinate function of the picture frame by ornamentally structuring the picture itself and integrating the frame. When Georges Seurat began to divide his representations into a system of dotted colours, he came up with a highly original version of ornamental image-making, and it is no accident that we find non-representational, marginal zones, reverberating like an echo of the composed scene. Although they grow out of the depths of the picture and thus still act as appendages, they seem to prefigure abstract painting whose subject matter was to become ornamentation itself.

In the meantime, Wassily Kandinsky introduced a mode of abstraction that returned a verdict on anything ornamental and decorative: form, according to Kandinsky, must grow out of inner necessity[2]. He thereby took the same direction previously proclaimed by Adolf Loos in his famous essay on ornament and crime[3]. With the advance of radical simplicity and purity of form, ornament inevitably sank into obsolescence. Loos even considered it a form of degeneration, a pathological outgrowth, hostile to civilisation. It took decades for ornament to be released from its banishment. Given the reductionism prescribed for American painting by Clement Greenberg, and the self-imposed pathos of spirituality among European exponents of l'art informel, any attempt to pursue the line of beauty was sheer sacrilege.

Wandlungen der Geometrie und des Ornaments - Zur Malerei von Jane Harris
Martin Hentschel

Ich denke, daß ein Bild vor allem ein Ornament sein sollte - Maurice Denis 1893[1]

I Das Unbehagen am Ornament

Auch wenn sich, wie Ernst Gombrich gezeigt hat, die abstrakte Kunst in ihren Anfängen einer nachhaltigen Auseinandersetzung um Ornament und Dekoration verdankte, so entledigte sich doch, einmal inthronisiert, sehr bald dieser ihrer Wurzeln. Das lag in der tradierten Verfassung des Ornaments als einer anhängenden Form begründet. Wie vielfältig und gewagt auch immer sein Vokabular ausfallen mochte, es war stets an eine Ordnung gebunden, die seine eigene Ordnungskriterien determinierte. Indem es eine architektonische Struktur bedeckte, verbarg oder pointierte es diese, aber als solches blieb es Zierrat: ein Detail, eine Nebensache. Auch im Hinblick auf die Organisation des neuzeitlichen Gemäldes war die applikative Funktion offensichtlich. Allein innerhalb der Rahmenleiste konnte sich das Ornament frei entfalten, doch war der Rahmen nicht notwendig mit ein und demselben Bild verknüpft. Er konnte von Besitzer zu Besitzer ausgetauscht werden.

Philip Otto Runge war womöglich der erste moderne Künstler, der die untergeordnete Funktion des Bilderrahmens aufwertete, indem er das Bild selbst ornamental strukturierte und darin das Rahmenornament integrierte. Georges Seurat lieferte, als er begann, alles Gegenständliche in ein System von Farbflecken zu dividieren, eine höchst originelle Version ornamentaler Bildlichkeit, und nicht von ungefähr finden wir in seinen Gemälden jene gegenstandsfreien Randzonen, die wie ein Nachklang der szenischen Komposition wirken. Obwohl sie aus dem Bildinneren erwachsen und ihm somit nach wie vor anhängen, muten sie wie ein Vorgriff auf eine abstrakte Malerei an, die das Ornamentale eigens thematisieren sollte.

Unterdessen trat mit Wassily Kandinsky eine Abstraktion auf den Plan, die über alles Ornametale und Dekorative ein Verdikt verhängte: Die Form, so postulierte Kandinsky, müsse "aus der inneren Notwendigkeit gewachsen" sein[2]. Damit vollzog er dieselbe Wende, die zuvor Adolf Loos in seinem berühmten Essay Ornament und Verbrechen proklamiert hatte[3]. Im Zeichen einer radikalen Schlichtheit und Reinheit der Form mußte das Ornament notwendig zur obsoleten Erscheinung absinken. Für Loos war es gar eine Form von Degeneration, pathologisch und zivilisationsfeindlich. Es sollte Jahrzehnte dauern, das

Not every art movement felt obliged to subscribe to the ideal of purification. Matisse charted a path that incorporated ornament as a self-evident factor in painting, and in his late period under the influence of jazz, Mondrian ultimately challenged his own phantasmagoria of severity which had penetrated every aspect even of his daily life. In England it was Bridget Riley, who exploited this freedom to give ornament a constitutive role in painting, in consequence of which her imagery was initially maltreated as patterns for fabrics and window displays.

II Geometry as a Playing Field

Jane Harris' paintings are based on three strict decisions that apply to her entire oeuvre. First, the ellipse is the basic form of her paintings; secondly, she uses only two colours per painting (though these may be mixed): one for the interior of the ellipse, the other for the surroundings; and thirdly, she applies a minimum of five coats of paint gradually building up the desired tone, whereby these layers are substantive participants in the phenomenon of the painting.

These criteria have little in common with the reductionism that issued from Greenberg's teachings and culminated in what was known as radical painting. On the contrary, Harris' paintings yield an unexpected richness of pictorial variation precisely because the artist restricts herself to these basic parameters. This applies first and foremost to the ellipse itself. As a geometric shape with two focal points, it is largely undetermined; it can on one hand bulge into a near circle and on the other taper into the thinnest of two-dimensional figures. Countless possibilities lie between these two extremes. The shape is also embodied by the archetypal figure of the mandorla. In medieval illumination, it figures as the aureole of light surrounding a holy person, frequently the figure of Christ, and in representations of the Ascension, for instance, it symbolises divine protection[4]. Undoubtedly the almond shape also refers to the vagina as the symbol of origin, and has, as such, retained its erotic implications to the present day in the formal vocabulary of advertising and design. Not that we are asked to associate Harris' work with the symbolic meanings of elliptical forms. Viewers may decide for themselves; but in some cases, as we shall see, the artist herself will invest a work with erotic meaning.

On the other hand she also uses the ellipse horizontally, as well as doubling, tripling and quadrupling the shape within a pictorial field. In addition, the edges almost always deviate from strictly geometric representation, for they are independent ornamental motifs, semi-elliptical in shape, that wreath the main figure. All kinds of arcs are possible here, even drop-like shapes that seem to be detaching themselves from their host. The curves may also become so complex that they acquire a resemblance to rocaille e.g. *Ripple*, (1999). The

Ornamentale aus seiner Verbannung zurückzuholen. Unter dem Reduktionismus, den Clement Greenberg der amerikanischen Malerei verordnete, und dem Pathos der Innerlichkeit, den sich das europäische Informel selbst auferlegte, mußte jeder Versuch, einer Ordnung der schönen Linie nachzugehen, wie ein Sakrileg erscheinen.

Nicht jede Kunstrichtung fühlte sich dem Purifikationsgedanken verpflichtet. Matisse etwa wies einen Weg, das Ornamentale ganz selbstverständlich der Malerei einzuverleiben, und der späte Mondrian, vom Jazz beeinflußt, relativierte letztendlich seine Phantasmagorien der Strenge, die bis in seinen alltäglichen Lebensraum eingedrungen waren. In England war es Bridget Riley, die diese Freiheit nutzte, um dem Ornamentalen einen konstitutiven Stellenwert in der Malerei zu geben, auch um den Preis, daß ihre Bilderfindungen anfänglich als Muster für Kleiderstoffe und Schaufensterdekorationen mißbraucht wurden.

II Geometrie als Dispositiv

Die Malerei von Jane Harris basiert auf drei strikten Entscheidungen, die sich durch sämtliche Arbeiten hindurchziehen. Die eine gilt der Ellipse als Grundform ihrer Malerei; die zweite läuft darauf hinaus, in einem Bild ausschließlich zwei Farbtöne zu verwenden (auch wenn diese gemischt sind): eine für das Innere der Ellipse, eine weitere für das Umfeld. Und drittens verwendet sie mindestens fünf Farbaufträge, die nach und nach zu dem gewünschten Farbton führen; die Farbschichtungen sind maßgeblich an den Phänomenen des Bildes beteiligt.

Dennoch haben diese Ordnungskriterien kaum etwas gemein mit jenen Formen von Reduktionismus, die aus der Greenbergschen Schule resultierten und in der Bewegung des radical painting ihre schärfste Ausprägung fanden. Im Gegenteil - gerade weil sich die Künstlerin auf jene basalen Voraussetzungen beruft, entfalten ihre Bilder einen ungeahnten Reichtum piktorialer Variabilität. Das betrifft allererst die Ellipse selbst. Als geometrische Form mit zwei Brennpunkten ist sie weitgehend nicht determiniert; sie kann sich einerseits dem Kreis annähern und andererseits bis hin zur extremen Zapfenform verjüngen. Innerhalb dieses Sprektrums bleiben zahllose Möglichkeiten offen. Darüber hinaus ist sie in einer archetypischen Form aufgehoben, der Mandorla. In der mittelalterlichen Buchmalerei repräsentiert diese die Aureole, die eine göttliche Erscheinung umgibt; sie tritt häufig bei Darstellungen der Majestas Domini auf; bei der Himmelfahrt Christi etwa symbolisiert sie den göttlichen Schutz[4]. Zweifellos ist in der Mandelform auch die Vagina - als Symbol des Ursprungs - mit beinhaltet, und dergestalt hat sie sich als erotische Anspielung im Formenrepertoire von Design und Werbung bis heute erhalten. Nicht daß wir aufgefordert wären, die symbolischen Bedeutungen der Mandorla angesichts

geometry can therefore be read more in the sense of a proposal than as a fixed criterion of order.

Harris' choice of the ellipse is also related to her wish to activate the entire pictorial surface. Because the ellipse has two focal points, we are prevented from fixing our gaze on a certain spot, and the artist's treatment of the edges locks into this feature of the elliptical shape. Her project is especially conspicuous in cases where the arcs change direction in one and the same ellipse. In *Rumba Bumba* (1999) the right side of the main shape is lined with near circular ellipses while the left is penetrated by a row of elongated ones. The resulting configuration subverts the clear relationship of figure and ground. While the protuberances on the right seem to rest on the pictorial ground, the longish ornamentation on the left covers part of the ellipse. The reading of figure and ground thus depends on where we focus our gaze. The artist has deconstructed the categorical definition of ornament as figure on ground: not only does the ellipse decorate the ground of the picture; the ground also embellishes the ellipse.

The complexity of the relationship is compounded by the closeness in colour values - different shades of umber - within and outside the geometric shape. Depending on the light, parts of the outside will seem darker than the inside and vice versa, and the sense of space will change as well. The paint and the light generate ceaselessly changing relations between dark and light, flatness and depth. We are confronted with a highly sophisticated form of what the German-American artist Hans Hofmann called the push-and-pull effect: the eye is pulled into the depths only to be pushed back up to the surface again, while at the same time experiencing constant changes in the colour values as well. The witty wordplay in the title *Rumba Bumba* (raw umber and burnt umber) draws our attention to this effect.

III The Iridescent Picture Surface

By now there is no mistaking the divergence between the works of Harris and those of the geometric abstraction that celebrated its resurrection in the eighties[5]. Geometry for Harris is a kind of matriarchal figure to whose guidance she appears to submit while in truth undermining it. And in her disobedience, Harris is indebted to an artist least likely to be ranked among the geometric abstractionists: René Magritte. Remember how Magritte punched an expanse of sky full of holes, totally upsetting the illusion; how he thrust the deepest space of his picture to the surface through a seemingly unmotivated, irrational protuberance. Interestingly enough, it was Josef Albers, who pursued a purified form of this play of spatial illusion in his Structural Constellations (1953-1958).

der elliptischen Formen bei Jane Harris mitzudenken. Das mag jeder Betrachter für sich entscheiden; wir werden aber sehen, das die Künstlerin selbst eine erotische Lesart im Einzelfall nahelegt.

Andererseits verwendet sie die Ellipse auch querliegend, und sie verdoppelt, verdreifacht und vervierfacht diese Form innerhalb eines Bildfeldes. Hinzu kommt, daß deren Randzonen eigentlich immer von der strengen Geometrie abweichen. Sie bilden eigene Schmuckmotive, die elliptisch bis halbkreisförmig das Hauptmotiv bekränzen. Alle Arten von Bögen sind hier möglich, bis hin zu Tropfenformen, die sich aus dem Ganzen herauszulösen scheinen. Auch können sich diese Bögen so komplex gestalten, daß die Ellipse in die Nähe einer Rocaille rückt z. B. *Ripple* (1999). Die Geometrie agiert also mehr im Sinne eines Dispositivs denn als feststehendes Ordnungskriterium.

Ohnehin hat die Wahl der Ellipse auch damit zu tun, daß Jane Harris bestrebt ist, die gesamte Bildfläche zu aktivieren. Aufgrund ihrer Bifokalität hindert die Ellipse den Betrachter daran, eine bestimmte Stelle zu fixieren, und ihre in den Bildern ausgearbeiteten Randzonen agieren in ebendiesem Sinne. Das gilt um so mehr, wo die Bögen innerhalb ein und derselben Ellipse ihre Richtung verändern. Bei *Rumba Bumba* (1999), beispielsweise finden wir die rechte Seite der aufragenden Großform mit einer Kette von Ellipsen besetzt, die einer Kreisform nahekommen, während die linke Seite von länglichen Ellipsen durchzogen wird, die aber umgekehrt in die Großform hineinzuragen scheinen. Dadurch wird die Eindeutigkeit einer Figur-Grund-Beziehung aufgehoben. Während die rechte Auskragung auf dem Bildgrund aufzuliegen scheint, ist es andererseits die linke Bildhälfte, die nunmehr über jene länglichen Randornamente einen Teil der Ellipse bedeckt. Figur und Grund verhalten sich also inversiv, je nachdem, welche Partie wir in Augenschein nehmen. Somit wird die kategoriale Bestimmung des Ornaments - Figur auf Grund - dekonstruiert. Insofern verhält sich nicht nur die Ellipse zum Bildgrund ornamental, sondern auch der Bildgrund zur Ellipse.

Die Phänomene werden weiterhin dadurch verkompliziert, daß die Farbe innerhalb und außerhalb der geometrischen Form - es sind verschiedene Umbratöne - nur geringfügig voneinander abweichen. Je nach Lichteinfall erschienen einmal Teile der Außenfarbe heller, ein andermal Teile der Innenfarbe, und dergestalt wechselt auch der räumliche Eindruck. Farbauftrag und Licht bewirken, daß die Differenzen zwischen hell und dunkel, Flächigkeit und Räumlichkeit niemals konstant bleiben. Wir haben es demnach mit einer sehr virtuosen Form jenes von Hans Hofmann elaborierten push and pull-Effektes zu tun: das Auge wird unentwegt in die Tiefe gezogen und andererseits von dort an die Oberfläche zurückgestoßen. In diesem Prozeß verwandeln sich permanent auch die Farbvaleurs. Der Bildtitel *Rumba Bumba* macht, indem

Harris exploits similar means of leading perception astray and generating uncertainty about what we see, beginning first and foremost with the ellipse. Even in some of the paintings where she comes close to her ideal geometric shape, as in *Croshe* (1999), we are seduced into a two-way reading: of an ellipse and of a circle depicted at an angle in the space of the picture. But when, as in *Crump* (1999), movement affects the ornamental zone to the right through the change in dimension of each successive curve, a spatiality is generated that makes one think of the virtual spaces painted into Baroque ceilings[6]. This interpretation is instantly undermined again by the evenly shaped rhythm of the ornament on the left edge of the ellipse, which enforces a flat reading.

I have already briefly mentioned another decisive factor involved in provoking such reactions: the application of the paint. From picture to picture, from inner form to outer form, Harris uses brushes of different widths. She applies her paint in short, regular intervals, generating within one formal continuum an even pattern that acquires added relief and/or uniformity with each new layer of paint. When she uses a different colour, Harris also changes the direction of her brushstroke.

If we take a frontal look at *Ish* (1997), we see the inside of the ornamental ellipse as a greenish-blue umber tone that is very close to black. There the brushstroke fades into the paint while the use of an even vertical gesture in the remainder of the painting makes the area outside the ellipse look dark violet. However, this impression is reversed when we approach the painting at an angle. The colouring of the ellipse now seems to be light blue-green, and its interior shows a vertical stroke. The mutation of phenomena, with many subtle intermediary stages depending on variations in the lighting, further destabilises the definition of the geometric shape within the space of the picture plane. Once again we find that the ellipse not only decorates the ground, but that the ground also decorates the ellipse. The ground has been activated as an independent form, an effect that is of course heightened by the counter-movement of the marginal ornamentation.

Where Harris uses a broader brush for the inside of an ellipse than for its surroundings, it appears to be more isolated. While the narrow stroke tends to be oriented more towards the picture surface, the broader stroke generates a kind of glazed relief, whose hills and dales are reversed depending on the light and the viewers angle of vision. *Full of Suspense* (1996/2000) offers a striking demonstration of this phenomenon. It is almost impossible for the viewer to distinguish dips and raised areas. The appearance of the colour literally lifts off from the paint as substance and forms an optical plane that keeps changing its position. No matter how material and tangible our impression

er zugleich die Farbbezeichnungen indiziert (raw umbra und burnt umbra), in witziger Weise auf diesen Effekt aufmerksam.

III Das Changieren der Bildoberfläche

Schon diese Bemerkungen deuten darauf hin, daß die Werke von Jane Harris nur wenig mit den Werken jener geometrischen Abstraktion gemein haben, welche Mitte der achtziger Jahre eine Wiederauferstehung feierten.[5] Die Geometrie bei Jane Harris ist eine Art Mutterfigur, deren Anweisungen nur scheinbar befolgt, in Wahrheit aber eher unterlaufen werden. Und bei diesem Ungehorsam steht ein Künstler Pate, den man am wenigsten in der Genealogie geometrischer Abstraktion vermuten würde: René Magritte. Erinnern wir uns, wie Magritte die Ansicht einer zusammenhängenden Himmelsfläche unversehens durchlöchert und damit die Illusion gänzlich umstülpt; wie er das räumlich Tiefste durch eine scheinbar unmotivierte, irrationale Auskragung unvermittelt in die vorderste Bildebene rückt. Interessanterweise war es Josef Albers, der mit seinen Strukturellen Konstellationen, 1953 - 1958, dieses Spiel mit der Raumillusuion in purifizierter Form fortsetzte. Ähnliche Möglichkeiten, die Wahrnehmung irrezuführen und eine Ungewißheit über das Zu-Sehende zu erzeugen, finden wir auch bei Jane Harris. Und das fängt abermals bei der Ellipse an. Schon in einigen jener Bilder, in denen sie sich ihrer geomerischen Idealform nähert z. B. *Croshe* (1999), sind wir verführt, eine doppelte Lesart anzulegen: die einer Ellipse und die eines in den Bildraum gedrehten Kreises. Wo aber, wie z. B. bei *Crump* (1999), die ornamentalen Randzone auf der rechten Seite eine Bewegung vollzieht, unter der sich das Maß jedes einzelnen Bogens verändert, da wird eine Räumlichkeit erzeugt, die nicht wenig an jene virtuellen Räume barocker Deckengemälde erinnert.[6] Andererseits wird diese Lesart sogleich relativiert, indem die linke Hälfte des Randornaments einen gleichförmigen Rhythmus erzeugt und dergestalt an die Flächenorganisation zurückgebunden wird.

Ein anderes, entscheidendes Moment, um derlei Irritationen zu provozieren, habe ich bisher nur beiläufig erwähnt: den Farbauftrag. Jane Harris benutzt von Bild zu Bild, von innerer Form zu äußerer Form, unterschiedlich breite Pinsel. Sie trägt die Pinselstriche in kurzen, gleichmäßigen Abständen auf und erzeugt so innerhalb eines Formenkontinuums ein gleichmäßiges Muster, das mit jedem Farbauftrag an Relief - oder/und an Homogenität - gewinnt. Mit dem Wechsel einer Farbe ändert sie auch die Richtung des Farbauftrags.

Betrachten wir etwa *Ish* (1997), aus einer frontalen Perspektive, so zeigt sich das Innere der ornamentalen Ellipse als ein grün-bläulicher Umbraton, der fast ins Schwarze übergeht. Der Pinselduktus löst sich in der Farberscheinung auf, während das übrige Feld, durch einen gleichmäßigen, vertikal gerichteten

of the paint may be, it eludes fixation, which also makes it so difficult to define the colours of the painting. This uncertainty is also indicated in the title, whose allusion to Hitchcock is no accident. It is amazing that we are faced with an abstract picture rather than the figurative scene implied in the title. Harris' paintings teach us to discover secrets even where nothing seems to be hidden.

The bifocal geometric shape bows to the polyfocal application of the paint in other works as well. The movement brought about by the colouring is not mimetic but emerges only in the eye of the beholder. The same thing applies to changes in the lighting, the more so when the paintings are illuminated from the side. The genealogy of such pictorial phenomena dates back to Pointillism and undoubtedly made its most aggressive appearance in Op Art. At stake here, and this also applies to Harris, is the lack of congruence between the facticity of the paint and its perception. The painting, as Max Imdahl puts it, becomes a musical score of seeing,[7] that must be played by the viewer. In contrast to Op Art, the eye of the beholder is certainly not physiologically taxed by Harris' paintings. Instead, rather like Albers, the artist produces a moderate optical irritation that requires body movement in order to be perceived and is moreover soothed by flashes of perception of the haptic surface texture.

An important contribution to this soothing effect is made by the border zone between the ellipse and the rest of the canvas. As a rule, it is specifically articulated in the form of an unbroken line, marking a third order of texture within the area of the picture. In *Ish*, for instance, the border provides a certain support in the iridescent appearance of the surface, and in *Oh Oh* (1999) it is emphasised with a broad outline that isolates the two ellipses in comic-like fashion. In *Full of Suspense* this zone fluctuates between flatness and depth, thereby infecting the inside of the ellipse as well. Moreover, the smaller the contrast of colour between the inside and the outside of an ellipse, the greater the impact of this intermediate zone - e.g. *Brune Brun* (1993) or *Skirt* (1999). However, the greatest visual irritation is caused by the surface effect when the texture of the ellipse closely resembles, indeed blends in with that of its surroundings, as in *Come Closer* (1996). The treatment of the border zone thus adds another spectrum to the wealth of pictorial detail.

IV Indicative Character, Titles and Association

One might assume that all of these phenomena, brought about by differences in the application of the paint and the geometric shape, are the result of extended research on the fundamental premises of the non-figurative picture and its perception. This would relate the work of Harris to the research undertaken by Josef Albers on colour and form in painting, or if one considers the sculptural shape, to the serial studies of Donald Judd. Both artists began

Duktus strukturiert, dunkelblau anmutet. Treten wir dagegen seitlich an das Bild heran, so verkehren sich Farb- und Faktureindruck beinahe diametral. Im Verhältnis zum Umfeld erscheint nun der Farbton der Ellipse hellbläulich, und wir gewahren ihr Inneres als eine horizontale Faktur. Die Mutation der Phänomene, die je nach Lichteinfall überdies viele Zwischenstufen einschließt, trägt dazu bei, die Verortung der geometrischen Form im Bildfeld zu destabilisieren. Hier zeigt sich erneut, daß nicht nur die Ellipse im Verhältnis zum Grund ornamental funktioniert, sondern auch der Grund im Verhältnis zur Ellipse. Der Grund wird als eigenständige Form aktiviert, und dazu tragen selbstverständlich auch die gegenläufig gerichteten Randornamente bei.

Wo eine Ellipse in ihrem Inneren mit einem breiteren Pinsel gemalt ist als die Umgebung, erscheint sie stärker isoliert. Während der schmale Pinselduktus eher an der Bildfläche orientiert ist, erzeugt der breitere Duktus eine Art gläsernes Relief, dessen Höhen und Tiefen je nach Lichteinfall und Betrachterperspektive wechseln. Sehr schön läßt sich dieses Phänomen etwa bei *Full of Suspense* (1996/2000), beobachten. Der Betrachter vermag kaum auszuloten, wo er es mit räumlichen Vertiefungen und wo mit Erhebungen zu tun hat. Die Farberscheinung löst sich buchstäblich von der Farbmaterie und bildet eine optische Ebene, die jedoch fortwährend ihre Position wechselt. So substantiell und greifbar die Farbe sich auch ausnehmen mag: sie entzieht sich jeglicher Fixierung. Das macht die Benennung der Bildfarben so schwierig. Auf diese Ungewißheit deutet schließlich auch der Bildtitel, der nicht von ungefähr an Hitchcock erinnert. Das Erstaunliche ist, daß wir uns doch einem abstrakten Bild gegenübersehen, und nicht etwa einer figurativen Szene, wie wir erwarten könnten, gingen wir vom Titel aus. Die Malereien von Jane Harris lehren uns, das Geheimnisvolle auch dort zu entdecken, wo scheinbar nichts verborgen ist.

Es gilt auch für andere Arbeiten, daß die Bifokalität der geometrischen Form überboten wird von der Polyfokalität des Farbauftrags. Die Bewegung, die durch die Bildfarbe entsteht, ist nicht mimetisch, sondern entsteht erst im Auge des Betrachters. Dasselbe läßt sich von den wechselnden Erscheinungen des Lichts sagen, die allerdings um so stärker zur Geltung kommen, je mehr die Bilder einer seitlichen Beleuchtung ausgesetzt sind. Die Genealogie derartiger Bildphänomene reicht bis in den Pointillismus zurück und fand in der Op Art sicherlich ihre aggressivste Ausprägung. Thematisch ist jeweils - und das trifft auch für Jane Harris zu - die Disidentität zwischen dem faktischem Farbauftrag und seiner Wahrnehmung. Das Gemalte selbst wird solchermaßen, um mit Max Imdahl zu sprechen, zu einer "Partitur des Sehens",[7] die erst vom jeweiligen Betrachter eingelöst wird. Im Unterschied zur Op Art wird das Auge des Betrachters durch die Bilder von Jane Harris keineswegs physiologisch überfordert. Die Künstlerin verwirklicht vielmehr, Albers vergleichbar, eine

Full of Suspense 1996/2000 Oil on canvas 117x64cm (Private collection)

gemäßigte optische Irritation, die wahrzunehmen der eigenen Körperbewegung bedarf und überdies stets von der punktuell sich einstellenden Wahrnehmung der Bildfaktur beruhigt wird.

Ein wichtiges Motiv dieser Beruhigung bilden jene Grenzzonen zwischen Ellipse und übrigem Bildfeld. Wo sie, wie das meistens geschieht, in Form einer durchgehenden Linie besonders artikuliert werden, da markieren sie eine eigene, dritte Ordnung innerhalb der Fakturen. Bei *Ish* zum Beispiel gibt die Grenzzone einen gewissen Halt im Verhältnis zu den wechselnden Oberflächenerscheinungen. Bei *Oh Oh* (1999), ist sie mit einem breiten Quast hervorgehoben, wodurch die beiden Ellipsenformen comicartig isoliert wirken. Bei *Full of Suspense* schwankt diese Zone zwischen flächiger und räumlicher Orientierung und affiziert so auch das Innere der Ellipse. Sie wirkt um so prägnanter, je weniger das Innere und das Äußere einer Ellipse farblich voneinander geschieden sind z. B. *Brune Brun* (1993) oder *Skirt* (1999). Wo sich die Faktur der Ellipse allerdings ganz an ihre Umgebung anlehnt wie bei *Come Closer* (1996), geht die durch die Oberflächenphänomene erzeugte Irritation des Auges am weitesten. So gesehen eröffnet der Umgang mit der Grenzzone ein zusätzliches Spektrum piktorialen Reichtums.

IV Anschaulicher Charakter, Titelgebung und Assoziation

Es könnte den Anschein haben, als seien all diese Phänomene, die aus den Differenzierungen des Farbauftrags und der geometrischem Form herrühren, Resultate einer lang anhaltenden Forschungsarbeit über die Grundbedingungen des gegenstandslosen Bildes und seiner Wahrnehmung. Das würde die Arbeiten von Harris in die Nähe jener Forschungen rücken, die Josef Albers im Hinblick auf Farbe und Form in der Malerei durchgeführt hat, oder, wenn man die plastische Form einbezieht, in die Nähe der seriellen Untersuchungen von Donald Judd. Beide Künstler gingen von einem streng limitierten Komplex formaler Grundentscheidungen aus. In der Tat scheinen diese kühlen und rationalen Methoden künstlerischer Arbeit einen gewissen Stellenwert bei Jane Harris einzunehmen.

Indessen betont die Künstlerin immer wieder, daß die Farbgebung ihrer Bilder auf Eindrücken beruht, die sie aus der alltäglichen Umgebung bezieht, seien sie unmittelbar präsent oder erinnert. Ein Indiz sind die Bildtitel; sie können, wenn auch oft sehr verhalten, jenen Realitätsbezug andeuten. Nehmen wir zum Beispiel *Pine* (1999), so evoziert die Farbkombination von Grün und Blau in Verbindung mit den grazilen Doppelformen zweifellos landschaftliche Assoziationen, die wiederum durch die Titelgebung ("Kiefer", "Föhre") gewissermaßen gesteuert werden. *Pine* hat darüber hinaus die zweite Bedeutung

with a rigorously restricted complex of formal decisions. This cool and rational approach to artistic work would indeed seem to play a role in Harris' method.

However, the artist always stresses the fact that colouring in her paintings is a consequence of immediate or remembered impressions drawn from her everyday environment. Her titles bear this out, for they indicate a relation to reality, however subtle it may be. Let us take *Pine* (1999) whose pairing of blue and green in combination with the graceful duplicate form no doubt evokes associations with a landscape. These are, to an extent, additionally influenced by the title, but the yearning contained in the verb to pine motivates still other readings inspired by the elongated ornamental arc of these ellipses. One might speak of what Hans Sedlmayr calls physiognomic qualities or indicative characters (anschauliche Charaktere), terms that refer to the intuitively comprehensible expression of forms regardless of whether they are figurative or not.[8] Physiognomic qualities transcend association; they lead to the elemental organisation of the work of art and thus to its form and colour. In consequence, linguistic equivalents generally fall short. We can only vaguely circumscribe how stepping out of a basically closed whole may have something to do with yearning as in the pointed arches of *Pine*, which, seen in reverse, are like barbs piercing the blue shapes. The indicative character is immediately evident, because it is basically pre-linguistic. Now and then such equivalencies of perceptual events may be heard in the sounds articulated by children. Finally, associative allusions and indicative characters can, of course, coincide as in the case of *Pine*, where one might envision an irresistibly blue sky shining between the branches of pine trees. But the moment we explicitly voice this idea, we have again distanced ourselves from the immediate perception of the picture and its physiognomic qualities.

By way of comparison, let us take a look at *Breeze* (1999), a painting formally related to *Pine* and also invested with the potential of scenic associations. All the more clearly do we realise that the vertical placement of the ellipses produces a different physiognomic quality, implied but not claimed by the title *Breeze* (or breezing in).

By working with double meanings that often reference heterogeneous contexts, Jane Harris substantially broadens the readings of her paintings. The indexical openness of the titles is especially conspicuous in those that make use of onomatopoeia, as in *Oh, Oh* (1999), *Ho Hum* (1998), *Mium Mium* (1996) and *La Di Da* (1994). But even then, specific meanings are not ruled out. For instance, a la-di-da person may be echoed in the latter painting through the composition of three similar ellipses, corresponding to the three syllables of the expression, and through physiognomic character as well, in the pretentious, almost affected appearance of the marginal embellishments. Thirdly, the slight

"sich sehnen", "vor Sehnsucht vergehen". Dies motiviert eine weitergehende Lesart, unter der die langgestreckten ornamentalen Bögen der Ellipsen besondere Aufmerksamkeit finden. Man kann hier, im Sinne Hans Sedlmayrs, von "physignomischen Qualitäten" oder "anschaulichen Charakteren" sprechen: diese Termini deuten auf den intuitiv erfaßbaren Ausdruck von Formen, unabhängig davon, ob diese gegenständlich oder ungegenständlich sind.[8] Die physiognomischen Qualitäten übersteigen das Feld des Assoziativen; sie führen in die basale Organisation des Kunstwerks und somit in die Form- und Farbgebung hinein. Dementsprechend bleiben die sprachlichen Äquivalente meist defizitär. Wir können nur vage umschreiben, daß das Heraustreten aus einem in sich geschlossenen Ganzen etwas mit "Sehnsucht" zu tun hat, wie es jene Spitzbögen bei *Pine* nahelegen, die umgekehrt gesehen wie Stacheln in die blauen Formen ragen. Der anschauliche Charakter ist unmittelbar evident, weil er eigentlich vor-sprachlich ist. Bisweilen kann man in der Lautartikulation von Kindern solche Äquivalente von Wahrnehmungsereignissen deutlicher erkennen. Schließlich können assoziative Anmutungen und anschauliche Charaktere durchaus zusammenlaufen, im Falle von *Pine* etwa in der Vorstellung eines unwiderstehlich blauen Himmels, der zwischen Kieferästen durchscheint. Allerdings - sobald wir diese Vorstellung deutlich aussprechen, entfernen wir uns schon wieder von der unmittelbaren Wahrnehmung des Bildes und seinen physiognomischen Qualitäten.

Betrachten wir im Vergleich die Arbeit *Breeze* (1999), die formal verwandt ist und zumal auch landschaftliche Assoziationen weckt, so gewahren wir um so klarer, daß die Vertikalität der Ellipsen eine andere physiognomische Qualität erzeugt, der von der Titelgebung ("Brise" bzw. breeze in - "fröhlich hereinschneien") zwar angesprochen, aber nicht eigentlich eingeholt wird.

Indem Jane Harris mit der Doppelbedeutung von Worten spielt, die oft heterogene Kontexte indizieren, erweitert sie die Lesarten ihrer Bilder beträchtlich. Die indexikalische Offenheit der Titel kommt insbesondere dort zum Tragen, wo diese mit bloßen Lauten *Oh Oh* (1999), *Ho Hum* (1998), *Mium Mium* (1996), *La Di Da* (1994) operieren, die im Sinne von Lautmalereien gelesen werden können. Aber selbst in diesem Bereich sind dezidiertere Bedeutungen nicht ausgeschlossen. So meint etwa im Englischen der Ausdruck "a la-di-da person" jemanden, der sich besonders vornehm, d. h. affektiert zu artikulieren versucht. Dies findet seinen Widerhall einerseits in der dreifach ähnlichen Ellipse - entsprechend der dreifachen Wortgliederung, und andererseits, wiederum auf physiognomischer Ebene, in dem prätentiösen, beinahe manierierten Auftreten der Randornamente. Drittens ist es nicht unwesentlich, daß die mittlere Ellipse ein wenig aus der Mittelachse verschoben ist. Dadurch entsteht eine leichte Bewegung unter den Ellipsen, die dergestalt an Sprechblasen erinnern, wie wir sie aus dem Comic kennen.

axial shift of the ellipse in the middle is not insignificant since it produces movement among the trio reminiscent of the speech bubbles in comics.

The titles do not always cover such a wide spectrum. *Bloody Mary* (2000) obviously calls to mind vodka and tomato juice, an association underscored by the combination of rousing colour and the delicate play of marginal forms. On spending more time with this painting, we find that the twice inverted ornamentation conveys an impression of rotation: as if we were under the influence of alcohol.

V Dissociative Modalities of Viewing

In general, the paintings of Harris are invested with considerable tactile qualities. The velvet surfaces not only manage to bundle, refract and bounce off the light; they also succeed in appealing to the viewers sense of touch. Their inimitable effect is, in fact, often due to the interplay between tactile and optical qualities. In extremely subtle terms, this also defines their parallel association with erotic appeal. And indeed there are works whose titles hint at the connection. For instance, when looking at *Come Closer* from the front, the ellipse looks as if it were behind its surroundings, which appear as a glistening, relief structure. But stepping closer and viewing the painting at an angle instead lends plasticity to the interior of the ellipse. These inversions of perception might be said to match what happens when coming closer to the skin of another person. Erotic stimulation changes the look of the skin, just as modifications in the viewing position change the effect of the painted surface.

In *Cul Noir* (1999), Harris makes no bones about provoking an erotic reading through the correlation of form and colour. Even though the artist herself says that *Cul Noir* is the name of a type of pig (cul noir = black ass) and also of a type of pottery made near Limoges,[9] hardly anyone, and certainly no male viewer, will be able to escape the idea of a vaginal or anal zone of the human body. The association is elicited by the fusion of ornamental shape and colour that fluctuates between wide-apart and willowy grace. On the dividing line between ornamental form and figurative shape, the painting no doubt recalls the far more explicit ornamental eroticism of John Wesley.

As we can see, the titles establish any number of relations to the reality of daily life, ranging from onomatopoeia, language games and metaphors to directly evocative meanings. Harris thereby achieves a degree of complexity, which in turn affects our study of her paintings. The frequently heterogeneous fields of meaning activate modalities of viewing, in which dissociatively superimposed layers offer ever new inspiration to the act of seeing. It is a

Nicht immer ist die Titelgebung so weit gefaßt wie in den letztgenannten Beispielen. Bei *Bloody Mary* (2000), zum Beispiel kommt uns unweigerlich jener verführerische Cocktail aus Tomatensaft und Wodka in den Sinn, und diese Imagination wird gleichermaßen durch die aufreizende Farbgebung wie durch das delikate Formenspiel des Randornaments evident eingelöst. Bei längerer Betrachtung stellt sich gar, vermittelt durch die zweifache Inversion der Ornamentierung, die Suggestion einer Drehbewegung der Ellipse ein: gleich so, als seien unsere Sinne infolge ausgiebigen Alkoholgenusses aus dem Lot geraten.

V Dissoziative Anschauungsmodalitäten

Grundsätzlich gilt, daß sich in der Malerei von Jane Harris in hohem Maße taktile Qualitäten realisieren. Die samtenen Oberflächen sind nicht nur fähig, das einfallende Licht zu bündeln, zu brechen und von dort aus zurückzuprojizieren, sondern ziehen nichtsdestoweniger auch den Tastsinn des Betrachters an. Ihre unverwechselbare Ausstrahlung verdankt sich oft gerade dem Wechselspiel zwischen taktilen und optischen Qualitäten. Dies bedingt - auf einer sehr subtilen Ebene - die Parallelität zu erotischen Reizen. In der Tat finden wir Arbeiten, die auch im Titel dieses Moment andeuten. Bei *Come Closer* etwa erscheint die Ellipse bei frontaler Betrachtung als eine Form, die räumlich hinter dem Umfeld liegt, welches als gleißende, erhabene Struktur zu Augen kommt. Tritt man näher und seitlich an das Bild heran, tritt dagegen das Innere der Ellipse plastisch hervor. Dieser prozessuale Umschlagseffekt entspricht in gewisser Weise der erotischen Annäherung an die Haut eines Menschen. Wie sich unter erotischer Stimulanz der Anblick der Haut verändert, so changiert die Bildoberfläche je nach Art und Weise ihrer Betrachtung.

Ganz unverhohlen wird die erotische Lesart bei *Cul Noir* (1999), in der Korrelation von Form und Farbe provoziert. Auch wenn, wie die Künstlerin selbst äußert, der Titel auf eine bestimmte Rasse von Schweinen mit ebendiesem Namen ("Schwarzer Arsch") zurückgeht, und andererseits auch eine spezielle Töpferei in der Gegend von Limoges meint,[9]: kaum jemand, und schon gar nicht ein männlicher Betrachter, wird sich der Vorstellung einer vaginalen oder analen, menschlichen Körperzone entziehen können. Dies wird ausgelöst durch die Verquickung von ornamentaler Form und Farbgebung, die zwischen Gepreiztheit und Grazie changiert. Auf der Grenze zwischen ornamentaler und figurativer Form, erinnert das Bild nicht wenig an die - ungleich deutlicheren - ornamentalen Erotismen eines John Wesley.

Wir sehen also an diesen Beispielen, daß die Titelgebung alle nur denkbaren Bezüge zur lebensweltlichen Realität herstellt. Sie reichen von Lautmalerei über Sprachspiele und Metaphern bis hin zu unmittelbaren evokatorischen

means of motivating beholders that links into the treatment in her paintings of the phenomena of colour and form.

By now it will have become quite clear that Harris' project must be seen as a rather distant relative of geometric abstraction, and that her works, with all their licence, perplexity and whimsy, actually show a distinct and highly specific affinity with the history of ornament. Geometry, as the other side of her painting, tends to serve as a springboard for the extremely daring pirouettes of Harris' art, leading to a rapprochement between geometric abstraction and ornament as they play their parts in the phenomena of the picture surface. To put it differently: geometry, the obvious factor, proves to be deceptive ground that may erupt at any moment, pulling the viewer into primeval depths. And yet, these depths have a way of turning into surface - the surface of ornament.

Translation: Catherine Schelbert

Bedeutungen. Dabei gewinnt Jane Harris einen Grad von Komplexität, der sich wiederum auf die Anschauung ihrer Bilder auswirkt. Insbesondere dadurch, daß die Bedeutungsfelder oft heterogen sind, werden Anschauungsmodalitäten hervorgerufen, die sich dissoziativ überlagern und solchermaßen das Sehen immer aufs Neue anspornen. Und diese Art der Motivation des Betrachters geht überein mit den dissoziierenden Phänomenen der Form- und Farbgebung.

Spätestens hier dürfte deutlich geworden sein, daß die Malerei von Jane Harris nur sehr bedingt einer Geschichte geometrischer Abstraktion zuzuordnen ist. Vielmehr ist in ihren Bildern auf eine sehr spezifische Weise die Geschichte des Ornaments aufgehoben und thematisiert - mit all ihren Freiheiten, Irritationen und Kapriolen. Die Geometrie - die andere Seite ihrer Malerei - hat eher die Funktion eines Sprungbretts, das die Künstlerin zu äußerst gewagten Pirouetten veranlaßt. Geometrische Abstraktion und Ornament werden schließlich in den Phänomenen der Bildoberfläche wechselseitig anverwandelt. Anders gesprochen: die Geometrie - das Offensichtliche - erweist sich als ein trügerischer Boden, der jederzeit aufbrechen kann, um den Betrachter in unvordenkliche Tiefen zu ziehen. Dabei kann sich herausstellen, daß die Tiefe auch eine Oberfläche sein kann - das Ornamentale.

Footnotes:

1. Maurice Denis, Théories, Paris 1913, quoted in: Ernst H. Gombrich, *The Sense of Order.* Oxford 1979, p. 58.

2. Wassily Kandinsky, Über die Formfrage in: *Der Blaue Reiter*, ed. by W. Kandinsky and F. Marc. Munich, 1912, reprinted in: Wassily Kandinsky, *Essays über Kunst und Künstler*, ed. and with a commentary by M. Bill, Bern, 1955, pp. 17 - 47, here: p. 23.

3. Adolf Loos, Ornament und Verbrechen (1908), in: *Sämtliche Schriften*, ed. by Franz Glück. Vienna, 1962.

4. Cf. Otto Brendel, Origin and Meaning of the Mandorla in: *Gazette des Beaux-Arts* (New York), 6th series, Vol. XXV, pp. 5 - 24.

5. Her approach to traditional geometric abstraction rather resembles the way in which David Reed or Jonathan Lasker treat traditional gestural abstraction.

6. The inner arc is de facto only the section of another ellipse with closer focal points.

7. Max Imdahl, Probleme der Optical Art: Delaunay - Mondrian Vasarely in: exh. cat. *Robert Delaunay*. Staatliche Kunsthalle Baden-Baden, 1976, pp. 19 - 35, here: p. 35.

8. It is an individual, indicative character that distinguishes one work from another…, that gives it a make-up which we are able to elucidate and formulate in words. In its broadest sense, the concept of character applies to all appearance. I can consider a colour in terms of its indicative character (its physiognomy) as much as I can a line, a substance, a landscape or a person. Such indicative characters are encountered everywhere in life. But in art, and only in art, do they become the foundation of works. Hans Sedlmayr, *Kunst und Wahrheit. Zur Theorie und Methode der Kunstgeschichte*. Mittenwald, 1978, p. 105. [italics by the author, transl. C.S.]

9. Letter from the artist to the author October 9, 2000.

Fussnoten:

1. Maurice Denis, Théories. Paris 1913, zit. nach Ernst H. Gombrich, *The Sense of Order.* Oxford 1979, dtsch: *Ornament und Kunst. Schmucktrieb und Ordnungssinn in der Psychologie des dekorativen Schaffens.* Stuttgart 1982, S. 70

2. Wassily Kandinsky, Über die Formfrage. in: *Der Blaue Reiter*, hrsg. von W. Kandinsky und F. Marc. München 1912, wiederabgedruckt in: Ders., *Essays über Kunst und Künstler*, hrsg. und komment. von M. Bill, Bern 1955, S. 17 - 47, hier: S. 23

3. Adolf Loos, Ornament und Verbrechen (1908), in: Ders., *Sämtliche Schriften*, hrsg. von Franz Glück. Wien 1962

4. Vgl. Otto Brendel, Origin and Meaning of the Mandorla, in: *Gazette des Beaux-Arts* (New York), 6th series, Vol. XXV, S. 5 - 24

5. Eher ähnelt ihre Art, mit der traditionellen geometrischen Abstraktion umzugehen, der Art, in der etwa David Reed oder Jonathan Lasker sich zur traditionellen gestischen Abstraktion verhalten.

6. De facto haben wir es bei dem inneren Bogen lediglich mit einem zweiten Ellipsenabschnitt mit näher gerückten Brennpunkten zu tun.

7. Max Imdahl, Probleme der Optical Art: Delaunay - Mondrian - Vasarely, in: Kat. *Robert Delaunay*. Staatliche Kunsthalle Baden-Baden 1976, S. 19 - S. 35, hier: S. 35

8. "Es ist ein individueller, anschaulicher Charakter, der ein Werk vom anderen unterscheidet …, ihm eine Eigenart gibt, die wir begrifflich zu erhellen und in Worten zu formulieren vermögen. In diesem weitesten Sinne findet der Charakterbegriff Anwendung auf Erscheinungen überhaupt. Ich kann ebenso eine Farbe nach ihrem anschaulichen Charakter (ihrer Physiognomie) auffassen wie eine Linie, einen Werkstoff, eine Landschaft oder einen Menschen. Solchen anschaulichen Charakteren begegnet man überall im Leben. In der Kunst aber, und nur in ihr, werden sie zur Grundlage von Werken." Hans Sedlmayr, *Kunst und Wahrheit. Zur Theorie und Methode der Kunstgeschichte.* Mittenwald 1978, S. 105 (Hervorh. ebenda)

9. Schreiben der Künstlerin an den Verfasser vom 9. Oktober 2000

Come Closer 1996 Oil on linen 66x91.5cm

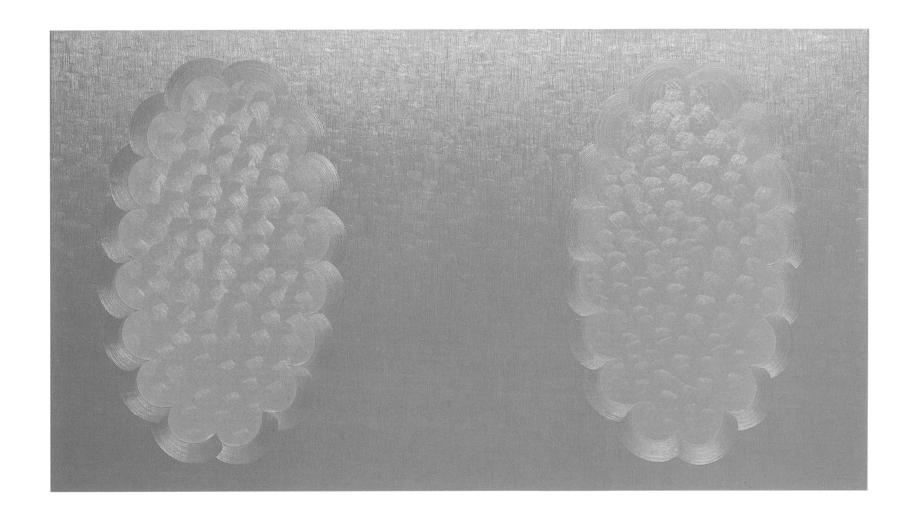

Oh Oh 1998 Oil on linen 71x127cm (Government Art Collection)

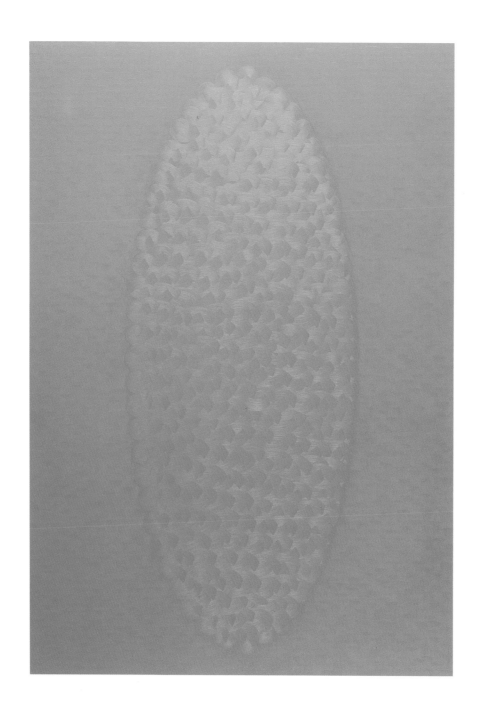

Croshe 1999 Oil on canvas 274x193cm

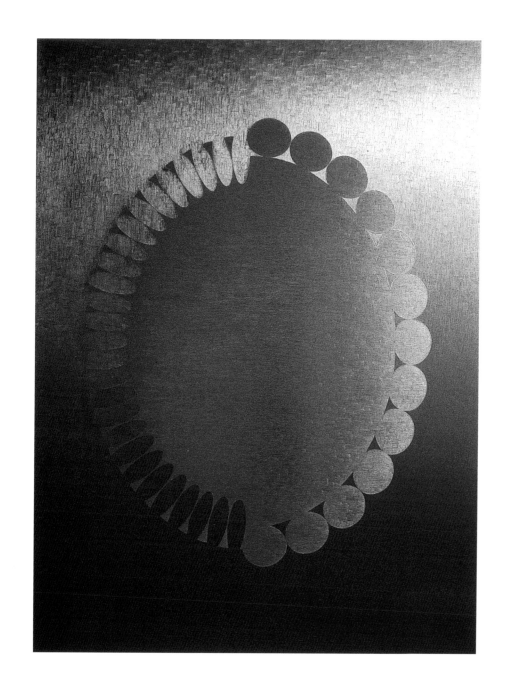

Rumba Bumba 1999 Oil on canvas 244x183cm

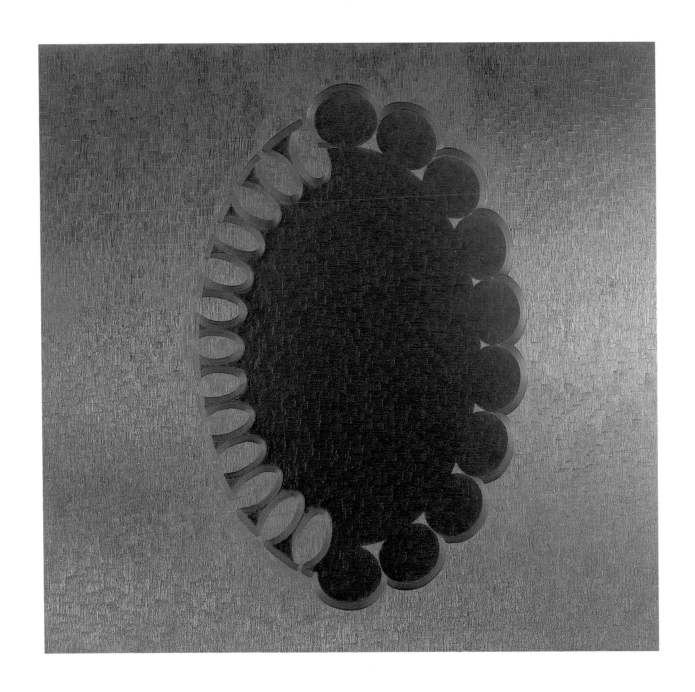

Ish 1997 Oil on canvas 122x127cm

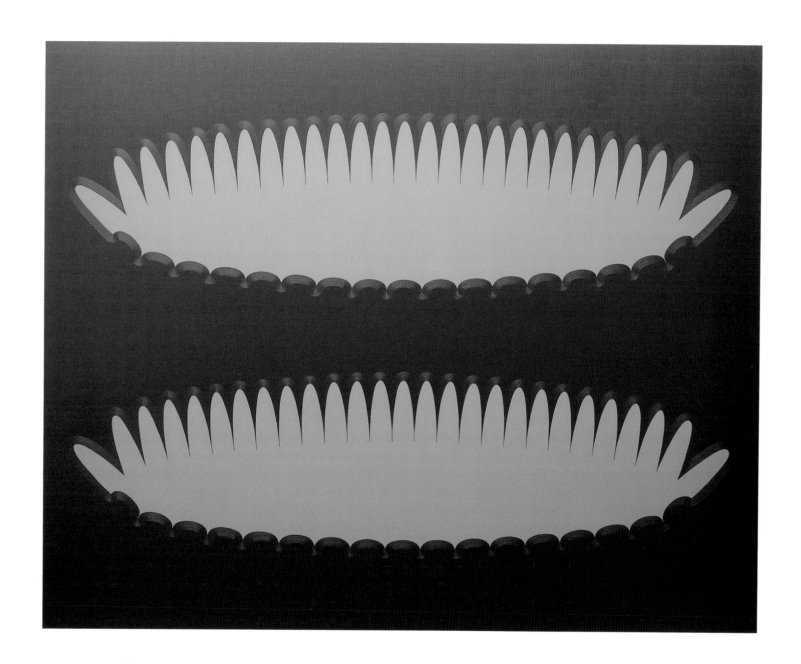

Pine 1998/9 Oil on canvas 193x244cm

Mium Mium 1996 Oil on linen 89x233.5cm

Skirt 1999 Oil on canvas 183x244cm

Breeze 1999 Oil on linen 87x64cm (Private collection)

Ripple 1999 Oil on canvas 153x168cm

Crump 1998 Oil on canvas 229x193cm

Well Well 2000 Oil on canvas 112x152cm (Private collection)

Cul Noir 1999 Oil on canvas 86.5x76cm

Jane Harris - Curriculum Vitae

Born Dorset 1956

1976-7	Camberwell School of Art
1977-79	Brighton Polytechnic, BA Fine Art
1979-81	Slade School of Art, Higher Diploma Fine Art
1989-91	Goldsmiths College, MA Fine Art

Solo Exhibitions since 1990

1992	Anderson O'Day, London
1994	Anderson O'Day, London
1996	Galerie Hollenbach, Stuttgart
	'Work in Progress', Camden Arts Centre, London
1999	Salle Attane, Saint-Yrieix-la-Perche, France
	Galerie Hollenbach, Stuttgart
2001	Southampton City Art Gallery
	Jack Shainman Gallery, New York
	Galerie Hollenbach, Stuttgart

Selected Group Exhibitions since 1990

1990	'Into the Nineties 2', Mall Galleries, London
1991	'Crossover', Anderson O'Day, London
1992	Riverside Open, London
	'Roll', Clove Building, London
	Whitechapel Open, London
	'East', Norwich Gallery, Norwich
	'The Discerning Eye', Mall Galleries, London
1993	'Maria Chevska, Kate Davis, Rachel Evans, Jane Harris', Anderson O'Day, London
	Jane Harris & Gerard Hemsworth, Powell Moya Partnership, London
	'Affective Light', Rear Window, London
	John Moores 18, Liverpool
1994	'Surface Tensions, Curwen Gallery, London
1995	'Das Abenteuer der Malerei', Stuttgart and Dusseldorf Kunstvereins
	John Moores 19, Liverpool (Prizewinner)
1996	'Out of Order': Independent Art Space, London
	'Really Out of Order': John Hansard Gallery, Southampton and touring
	'About Vision: New British Painting in the1990s'; MOMA, Oxford and touring
	'small truths'; John Hansard Gallery, Southampton and touring
1997	'Finish' (with Ian Davenport, Alexis Harding, Jason Martin), Spacex Gallery, Exeter
	'Jerwood Painting Prize' (Shortlisted), Lethaby Gallery, London
	'Jahresgaben'; Kunstverein Stuttgart
1998	'Ecstasy', Jack Shainman Gallery, New York
	'Ten British Painters', Galerie Hollenbach, Stuttgart
	'Eliminate the Negative', Gasworks Gallery, London
1999	Jane Harris & Ana Prada, Anderson O'Day, London
	'La Casa, Il Corpo, Il Cuore', 20th Century House, Museum of Modern Art Foundation Ludwig, Vienna; touring to Museum of Modern Art, Prague (2000)
	'Sublime: The Darkness and the Light', Arts Council Touring Exhibition, John Hansard Gallery, Southampton
2000	'Simon Callery, Jane Harris, Mandy Ure, Roy Voss - Recent Paintings', Djanogly Gallery, Nottingham
	'Force Fields', Hayward Gallery, London
	Cheltenham Drawing Exhibition (Prizewinner), Cheltenham and touring
2001	'Again, Again', John Hansard Gallery, Southampton (Curating and exhibiting)

Bibliography

1991	Nick de Ville, The Independent, December 17
1992	Robin Dutt, 'Jane Harris', What's On, July 29-August 5
	John McEwen, 'Jane Harris', The Sunday Telegraph, July 5
	Tim Hilton, The Guardian, June 25
	Adrian Searle, 'Jane Harris', Time Out, July 1-8
1993	Tim Hilton, The Independent, May
	Tim Hilton, The Independent, October 24
	Lewis Johnson, 'In the Light of Questions of Place', Catalogue Essay for 'Affective Light'
1994	David Lillington, 'Affective Light', Time Out, December 29-January 5
	Simon Morley, 'Jane Harris', Art Monthly, June
	Sue Hubbard, 'Jane Harris', Time Out, May 18-25
	Adrian Dannatt, 'Jane Harris', Flash Art International, October
	Nick de Ville, 'Jane Harris', Catalogue Essay
1995	Dr Gerhard Charles Rump, Die Welt, June 14
	Hans-Joachim Muller, Die Zeit, June 9
1996	Stuart Morgan, 'Out of Order', Catalogue Essay
	Nick de Ville, 'small truths', Catalogue Essay
	'The Vision Thing', Andrew Wilson, Art Monthly , Dec 96 -Jan 97
	William Feaver, The Observer, November 17
	Philip Hensher, Mail on Sunday, November 17
	Tim Hilton, Independent on Sunday, November 17
1997	Godfrey Worsdale, 'small truths', Art Monthly, March
	Maite Lores, 'small truths', Contemporary Visual Arts, Issue 14, April
	Judith Bumpus, 'Jerwood Painting Prize', Catalogue Essay
1998	Nicholas de Ville, 'Ways of Seeing and the Pleasure of the Visual', Contemporary Visual Arts, Issue 18, April
	'Art forum berlin' Dr Gerhard Charles Rump, Die Welt, October 2
	'Breites Spektrum, Englische Kunst bei Hollenbach' Stuttgarterzeitung, November
1999	Martin Coomer, 'Jane Harris, Ana Prada', Time Out, April
	Keith Patrick, 'Jane Harris at Galerie Hollenbach' Contemporary Visual Arts, Issue 23, June
	Stephen Foster, 'La Casa, Il Corpo, Il Cuore', Catalogue Essay
	Christopher Kool-Want, 'Sublime - The Darkness and the Light', (The Sublime Now - Language), Catalogue Essay
2000	Martin Herbert, 'Simon Callery, Jane Harris, Mandy Ure, Roy Voss', Catalogue Essay
	Simon Wallis - Interview in the above catalogue

Public Collections

Arthur Andersen Art Collection, Arts Council of England, The Boise Collection, Brighton Polytechnic, British Airways, Department of Trade & Industry, GlaxoWellcome, Goldsmiths MA Collection, Government Art Collection, Sacker & Partners, SAKS Fifth Avenue

Acknowledgements:

Anderson O'Day Fine Art, 5 St Quintin Avenue, London W10 6NX

GALERIE HOLLENBACH
70192 Stuttgart, Ganghoferstrasse 28

SouthamptonCityArtGallery:

Photography: Peter White, FXP Photography

Design: Nick de Ville

Printed by the Furnival Press, 61 Lilford Road, London SE5 9HR

Published 2001

With special thanks to:

Jiri Kratochvil
Kok Boon Lim
Gary Simmonds
Magdalena Wisniowska

ISBN No: 0 901723 26 6

(cover: detail of *Full of Suspense* illustrated on page 18)